Building
Bridges

REtoday
Services

by Julia Ipgrave

Building e Bridges

REtoday Services

RE Today Services, a part of Christian Education, is an ecumenical educational charity which works throughout the United Kingdom.

Its aims are:

- to support Religious Education in schools;
- to increase awareness of the spiritual, moral, social and cultural dimensions of the curriculum;
- to articulate Christian perspectives on education.

RE Today Services is committed to the teaching of the major world faiths in Religious Education, and to an accurate and fair representation of their beliefs, values and practices in all its teaching materials.

RE Today Services fulfils these aims:

- by publishing teaching materials like this book and background papers together with a termly magazine *REtoday* and the *British Journal of Religious Education*;
- by offering professional development and consultancy services through its professional staff;
- by arranging national and regional courses for teachers, pupils and others interested in education;
- by research and curriculum development work;
- by supporting the Professional Council for Religious Education and distributing its journal *Resource*.

Thanks to a number of colleagues, in particular Andrew Raine from Birmingham, Paul Archdeacon, Keith Culverwell, Jane Gadsby from Leicester, and Charlotte Gravestock from East Sussex, for the ideas and practical support they have given to the development of the ***building e-bridges*** *project.*

Written by Julia Ipgrave

Cover design by Christian Education Publications

Designed and typeset by Christian Education Publications

Published by
Christian Education Publications
1020 Bristol Road
Selly Oak
Birmingham
B29 6LB

British Cataloguing-in-Publication Data
A catalogue record for this book is available from the British Library.

ISBN 0-904024-54-8

First published 2003

Printed and bound by Henry Ling, Dorchester

Introduction: Bridging the gap

Towards the end of the 1990s, two Leicester schools took advantage of their newly appointed computer suites to embark on an e-mailing project that would bring their pupils together in an inter-faith, intercultural partnership. One of the schools was an inner city junior school serving a predominantly Muslim community, and the other a suburban Catholic primary school. During the first year the schools developed a model of pupil-to-pupil dialogue by e-mail which has now become a key component of the schools' RE and ICT programmes of study for Year 5 and 6 students.

Since these early days of the **building e-bridges** project, educational developments, national and international events have given new urgency to the work of bringing children together across religious, ethnic and cultural divides and placed such encounter between differences at the forefront of the fight against prejudice and for social harmony. The project has expanded to embrace a number of primary schools in an inter-authority link between Leicester and East Sussex, and has continued to grow as other schools across the United Kingdom see in e-mail exchange an answer to some of the questions our modern world raises about the education of its children.

In this resource we aim to set out a model of inter-faith dialogue by e-mail for interested teachers to consider or adapt for the needs of their own schools. It will lay down the principles that have guided existing work in the field, offer advice on the practicalities of setting up e-mail partnerships and suggest a variety of ways in which the links might be developed further.

Contents

Four reasons for building e-bridges

Planning, running and maintaining an e-mail dialogue requires a degree of hard work, commitment and enthusiasm. It is important, then, that any teacher embarking on such a project is convinced of the value of the enterprise. Below are four good reasons for getting involved.

Religious Education

The multi-faith Religious Education taught in our schools requires pupils not only to reflect on and express their own experiences, understandings and beliefs, but also to relate to the experiences, understandings and beliefs of others. When the reflecting and relating are brought together, Religious Education becomes a dialogue between self and other. The government's curriculum agency, the Qualifications and Curriculum Authority (QCA) guidance for Religious Education promotes such dialogue when it encourages consideration of different points of view, discussion of own and other people's values, thinking about own and other people's ideas of what is right and wrong (QCA, 2000). That dialogue can become more meaningful where it is a dialogue between people and not just between pupils and the pages of a book.

Discussion between children in any class will involve a dialogue of different viewpoints and experiences, but many Religious Education teachers wish to introduce their pupils to a greater diversity of cultures and faiths than the demography of their school allows. While some schools reflect the rich cultural and religious diversity of twenty-first century Britain, many of our schools (in inner cities, suburbs, council estates, villages) are relatively homogeneous with more limited opportunity for dialogue. Forming e-mail links between schools, across cities or in different regions of the country, is one way to engineer a fruitful encounter with difference. Careful pairing of schools and pupils can bring together diverse religious experiences and perspectives in inter-faith dialogue.

- Jemma has never met a Hindu before but now finds herself engaged in meaningful discussion with Bhavisha about what happens when we die.
- Natalie tells Asiya that she went on a skiing holiday with her family at half term. Asiya gives her a detailed description of her own experience of going on *Hajj*.
- Ahmed thought that someone who didn't believe in God was necessarily a bad person until he exchanged views on justice and forgiveness with Matthew, his e-mail friend.
- Balvinder from the inner city has an interesting debate on the rights and wrongs of fox hunting with Dominic who lives in fox hunting country.
- Sarah knew that angels brought the message of Christmas. She didn't know, until Fahima told her, that they also brought the message of the Qur'an.

Citizenship

The QCA guidance on Religious Education clearly states that an aim of the subject is to prepare young people for 'life as citizens in a plural society' (QCA 2000:2), and so the link is made between RE and the new curriculum subject of Citizenship. From the QCA guidance on Citizenship, we learn that a good citizen needs knowledge, skills and understanding. Pupils need to know more about their community, their country and their world if they are going to become effective citizens of all three. Part of that knowledge means awareness of diversity (including religious diversity) in a plural society. Pupils also need to develop the participatory skills requisite for the exercise of healthy democracy. These skills include discussing with others, explaining personal views and opinions, debating topical issues (QCA 1999, *The National Curriculum*, PSHE and Citizenship, Key Stage 2).

Both knowledge and skills can be enhanced through e-mail partnerships:

- As children from the inner city converse with children from the suburbs or the council estates, as children from urban locations communicate with those living in more rural settings, they learn about 'the differences and similarities between people', about 'people living in other places … and people with different values and customs' (QCA and DfES, 1999, *PSHE and Citizenship*, Key Stage 2, 4f, 4b).
- As children read what their partners have written in their e-mails and formulate their responses, they learn to discuss and debate (QCA and DfES, 1999, *PSHE and Citizenship*, Key Stage 2, 2a).
- As children tackle issues such as violence and homelessness, the rights of animals and care for the environment, they consider the social and moral dilemmas of modern life (QCA and DfES, 1999, *PSHE and Citizenship*, Key Stage 2, 5g).

An e-mail from Year 6 pupils

We've been thinking a bit more about homeless people and we actually feel quite strongly about them.

When we see homeless people we feel sorry for them because if we were them we would feel very afraid and upset. So every time we see a homeless person we stop and think about them. We think the government could help by giving them a shelter and some clothes and a bit of advice. So that they can get up and do something in life instead of sitting and moping around. Because everyone has a talent.

We were wondering what you feel about homeless people?

Please reply soon.

By Amira and Mohsin

Community cohesion

In guidance for RE and Citizenship, a positive approach to diversification is expressed. Alongside this is real concern that difference of religious and cultural identity may be a cause of fragmentation in our society. The reports by the Ministerial Group and the Independent Review Teams on Public Order and Community Cohesion (Home Office 2001a, 2001b) warned of the fracturing of some English towns along racial, cultural and religious lines (2001a 1.6, 8). They recommended that schools should help counter the segregation of communities from each other by 'developing contacts with other cultures' (2001b 5.8.3) and 'inter-school twinning' (2001b 5.8, 12). Schools wishing to follow these recommendations might find e-mail links an excellent way of establishing a twinning relationship. The breaking down of barriers and building up of cross-cultural friendships might start with something as simple and natural as a friendly exchange about the food we eat.

Part of an exchange between Year 6 pupils

Hi it's us again, we don't celebrate Christmas so we don't have Christmas dinner. We normally have Indian food such as chicken biryani and curry with spices in it the food is very filling and delicious.

By the way have you tasted Indian food?

From Amira and Mohsin

Hi,

Yes we have tried Indian food from a take away, but that is probably not the same as home cooked food...

Information and Communication Technology

During the course of a year's programme of e-mail exchange there are a number of ICT skills children might develop. These include:

- word processing;
- opening and sending e-mails;
- opening and sending attachments;
- use of digital camera and webcam;
- video conferencing.

The technology used can be as complex or as simple as the children (and teachers) are ready for, but the key ICT learning point of the project is that communication technology can be used to serve other needs and solve other problems.

One of the emphases of the National Curriculum guidance on ICT is that it should be seen as a tool that enables things to happen. It states that pupils should 'learn how to employ ICT to enable rapid access to ideas and experiences from a wide range of people, communities and cultures' (QCA 1999, p96). A cross-cultural, inter-religious e-mail link, such as we are describing, fits exactly into this aim. The National Curriculum also tells us that pupils should be given opportunities 'to apply and develop their ICT capability through the use of ICT tools to support their learning in all subjects' (QCA 1999, p39). Teachers of RE looking for a way to involve ICT in the delivery of this subject can find an answer in **building e-bridges**.

A case study of inter-faith dialogue

Uplands Junior School in Highfields, inner city Leicester, and St Thomas More Catholic Primary School in a more suburban area of the same city were obvious candidates for an e-mail link. Both had a school population where over 90% of the pupils were affiliated to and actively participating in one faith tradition, whether at home, mosque, church or school.

Teachers at the two schools were looking for ways of widening their pupils' perspective on faith issues. In this they were prompted by the Leicestershire Agreed Syllabus used at Uplands and the Catholic Diocese of Nottingham which actively encourages its schools to engage with other faiths. In both cases the schools were looking for an approach to learning about other faiths that respects the integrity of the children's own faith as they encounter alternative viewpoints in Religious Education lessons and also breaks down barriers to learning posed by prejudices children may have acquired about religious difference. In religious dialogue the pupils are constantly drawing on their own faith position as they relate to the viewpoints of their partners.

At the beginning of the link the Religious Education co-ordinators met together to share the schools' RE schemes of work based on the local agreed syllabus and the Catholic diocesan syllabus respectively. From these they drew a number of termly themes that would be used with the Year 5 and Year 5/6 classes taking part. Pupils were paired, trying to match them as far as possible according to ability. The e-mailing started in October, initially as a continuous dialogue between the pupils, with children responding to their partners as they received e-mails from them.

The experiences of the first year provided several valuable lessons for future development of the project. Most importantly they confirmed the value of such a project for the children's learning and social development. These positive aspects were advertised in reports written by the RE co-ordinators at the end of the year.

The St Thomas More perspective

This initiative offered the exciting possibility for children to take responsibility for their own learning, asking the questions that were relevant to them.

From the outset of the project the children have always eagerly looked forward to communicating with their 'partners', whom they quickly came to call 'friends'.

The exchanges have meant that the children have had a real audience. They have had to 'think through' things they might otherwise have taken for granted. They have had to try to express themselves in a meaningful way.

The Uplands perspective

The sense of 'friendship' has been key to the e-mail experience. For our pupils, having an e-mail partner, knowing their name, their interests, something about their family and their life, has been like having their special friend.

As well as learning about others, the children have been reflecting on their own beliefs, principles, preferences, and learning to express these to their partners.

It has been an opportunity for them to bring their wider experiences to school and see them valued there.

Other forms of electronic communication were trialled during the year and proved successful. The children took photographs of each other using digital cameras, and sent these as attachments to their e-mail partners. The last communication of the year involved sending video clips of the children talking to their partners using the webcam.

> There was great excitement when photographs of their friends arrived by e-mail, and even more when they could see and hear their partners talking to them on video clips.
>
> **End of year project report: Uplands**

The grand finale of the year's exchange was a face-to-face meeting between the pupils when they met in a city park for a picnic and games afternoon. The first activity of the park visit was for the children to use the digital photos they had received to try and track down their partners.

The first year of the project also raised some problems which led to improvement. Logistically it revealed some weaknesses in the set-up of the ICT suite at Uplands. The computer suite had originally been planned to enable whole-class teaching with a focus on the whiteboard. It was reorganised for more independent work, with easy movement between the computer stations for teachers and other staff supporting the dialogue.

> Our children are greatly looking forward to meeting their 'partners' at the park in July. A tremendous number of parents have volunteered to accompany the group, displaying the support that they give the project.
>
> **End of year project report: St Thomas More**

The flexible timetabling of the e-mailing meant that it was harder to synchronise the sending and receiving of e-mails. Several times pupils opened up their e-mail accounts only to be disappointed to find no reply waiting for them. The timing also meant that it was sometimes difficult to tie in the e-mail discussion with class RE work. It was as a result of this experience that the schools adopted a more structured approach for the following year with discrete blocks of exchange each with their own focus, and timetabled to take place during specific weeks over the three terms[1].

As the project moved into its second year, it became embedded in the schools' Improvement (or Development) Plans and an important contributor to an ethos in both schools of openness to the community and respect for diversity. In addition to the activities described above, the schools developed their link further by exchanging assemblies.

> We have learned that other schools have a lot of different religions. We have also learned that people are different, but that doesn't mean we should tease them. We should respect everyone because they are our brothers and sisters.
>
> **Pupil from St Thomas More**

Children from St Thomas More have contributed to Uplands children's Religious Education by bringing a Christingle assembly and a presentation on the theme of Epiphany to the school. Uplands children have taken assemblies on Hajj and on an Islamic view of Creation to their Catholic neighbours. After each performance the children were able to socialise, with a shared play time.

[1] See page 23, 'Timetabling the programme of exchanges'

> After September 11 our children didn't link the terrorists with the Muslim children at Uplands. The project has shown them that Islamic children are as normal as they are.
>
> **RE co-ordinator, St Thomas More**

One of the positive features of the developing relationship between the two schools has been the interest of parents. The shared assemblies and park visits have been occasions that parents and some governors have attended. For them as well as for their children, the link has given opportunities for a positive encounter with difference.

> I used to think our religions were really different, but they're not. Before I used to think that Christians believe in their own religion and I believe in mine, but now I like both because there isn't much difference.
>
> **Pupil from Uplands**

Another development was the planning of a Places of Worship Day, whereby a group of pupils from Uplands took some of their friends around a local mosque, explaining the features of the building and the worship that takes place there. The children took photographs of the mosque and then returned to Uplands ICT suite to convert these into a guide to the building. At the same time another group of pupils from both schools took part in a parallel programme at St Thomas More church with follow-up activities in St Thomas More ICT suite.

> The project made Christians seem like real people. We use different names for our gods and prophets, but it's the same god and many of the prophets are the same.
>
> **Pupil from Uplands**

At a time when so much is said about conflict between the perspectives and people of different faiths, staff at these two schools trust that they are making a positive contribution to bridging some of the cultural and social divides.

Dimensions of dialogue

Dialogue is very much in fashion as an educational tool. We have already noted the importance of dialogue to Religious Education and Citizenship. It also has a prominent place in cross-curricular programmes designed to promote both emotional literacy and thinking skills within our schools. Dialogue involves the interaction of ideas and of the people who hold those ideas; it is at the same time an intellectual and a social activity. Both aspects are recognised in the thoughts on dialogue recorded on this page. Both play an important role in e-mail exchange.

Thoughts on dialogue

Dialogue is not a battle with winners and losers but is a way of enquiry into what is right, true and of value, in partnership with others. **Robert Fisher, in *Teaching Children to Think* (Nelson Thornes, 1990)**

Dialogues could be described as cultural tools for thinking – the form has been developed by generations of writers and lies waiting to be exploited in education today. **Steve Williams, from 'Artful Dialogues' in *Teaching Thinking* (Autumn 2002)**

The consequence of genuine dialogue is the realisation that one is valued for what one does, thinks and says. **Joanna Haynes, in *Children as Philosophers* (Routledge/Falmer, 2002)**

The thing about [classroom dialogue] is you know it's not just ideas but the ideas belong to someone so you can't just say, 'That's rubbish!' That's not kind. You have to think a bit about it instead. **Sara, aged 11**

Dialogue makes the most of our differences. It creates the opportunity for everyone to learn from encounter between ideas that do not immediately agree. Through dialogue emerges the pleasure of engaging playfully with contrast, contradiction and puzzlement. **Antidote, from 'Dialogue: making meaning together' in *The Quality of Learning: An Emotional Literacy Handbook* (2002)**

Electronic dialogue

When we think of dialogue as an educational tool we usually think of class discussion, but dialogue also has its written form. Since the Ancient Greeks, written dialogue has been a vehicle of philosophical and theological argumentation. E-mail dialogue is somewhere between the two forms: it is a genuine to-and-fro of ideas between individual dialogue partners, but it is also written. Though it may try to reproduce as closely as possible the spontaneity and relational quality of speech, electronic communication cannot have quite the intimacy and immediacy of face-to-face encounter.

E-mail dialogue does have some advantages over oral debate, however. While in class or group discussions there is a danger of a few children dominating, *all* the children engaged in e-mail dialogue have an equal chance to make their views known. *All* are required to think. *All* will have their contribution recognised and valued as they earn a reply from their appointed e-mail partner. For younger participants, who may not be as quick as adults at processing dialogue, e-mail provides valuable thinking time. The process gives them space to reflect on their partner's words and marshal their thoughts before they formulate a response.

Religious dialogue

The value of dialogue to pupils' Religious Education has been recognised on page 4, but the religious content of the e-mail exchanges does raise issues that need careful consideration. Dialogue is valued as a tool of liberal education: it contributes to the development of a questioning, critical classroom culture. Yet this very questioning and criticism might appear a threat to the religious loyalties of young minds. Will they become confused as they encounter the contrasting views and beliefs of other faith stances? Will their own faith (or secular position) be shaken?

These are genuine concerns, but the premise on which the 'building e-bridges' model is founded is that encounter with difference is inevitable. Young people meet an increasing variety of viewpoints as travel and communication technology improve. As teachers, we can help pupils position themselves within such a plural and fluid society and encourage them to adopt a confident and positive (as opposed to suspicious and confrontational) approach as they engage with difference. Pupils need to be trained in the skills of dialogue.

In religious dialogue, pupils are:

- starting from their own faith perspective (or secular position) with opportunities to express their own beliefs and present their own practices.
- learning that those of other faiths (and none) are people very like themselves, a lesson which helps to reduce prejudice and suspicion of other traditions.

In recognition of the sensitive nature of religious dialogue, the original Leicester e-mail partnership turned to the advice on Christian-Muslim dialogue given in a series of supplements for parish newsletters and schools by the Committee for Other Faiths of the Bishops' Conference for England and Wales. The supplements were designed to 'help Catholics deepen their faith by promoting greater awareness of other faiths through prayer and action in the light of the Church's teaching'.

The fourfold classification of dialogue[1] used in these supplements is of general application to encounter between different faith and life stances:

- **Dialogue of Life** – ordinary human experience of respect and friendship;
- **Dialogue of Action** – working together for justice and common ethical and social objectives;
- **Dialogue of Religious Experience** – sharing spiritual riches;
- **Theological Dialogue** – discussing questions of belief.

Stages of dialogue

One of the difficult things about maintaining e-mail partnerships between children is taking the dialogue beyond the initial stages of chat and giving it a structure and a purpose. The aim of the 'building e-bridges' model is to promote an exchange that ties in with Religious Education and Citizenship objectives and incorporates a progression of dialogue skills. The stage-by-stage model that has developed is influenced by the fourfold classification of dialogue set out above. In the table on the next page, four stages are set out with some examples of questions that could be explored at each stage. As children engage in e-mail dialogue they might bring together more than one stage (accounts of Christmas celebrations, for example, might involve discussion of belief as well as practice), but if teachers are aware of all four in their planning and support, they can ensure progression.

[1] As proposed by the Vatican's 'Secretariat for non-Christians' (subsequently renamed the Pontifical Council for Inter-Religious Dialogue) in a 1984 document, *The Attitude of the Church towards the Followers of Other Religions: Reflections and Orientations on Dialogue and Mission*

Stage of dialogue	Examples of questions that could be explored
Introduction (Dialogue of Life) • Self-presentation • Getting to know each other • Building friendship	Do you enjoy going to school? Why or why not? What are you especially good at? What do you do after school? What do you like doing in your spare time? Do you have any ideas of what you would like to do in the future? Who do you live with? Do you have any particular jobs you have to do in your home? Do you like living where you do? Why or why not? Who is your best friend and what makes them such a good friend?
Sharing experience (Dialogue of Experience) • Describing and explaining one's own practices • Finding out about each other's practices • Gathering information • Comparing experiences	Are there any times of year that are particularly special to you? Why are they special? What do you do to celebrate them? Did you celebrate Christmas? How? Is Ramadan an important time for you? How are you marking it? Do you have a book that is special to you? Do you have a place that is special to you? Do you attend any place of worship? What do you do there? How do you welcome a new baby into your family or community?
Ethical debate (Dialogue of Action) • Debating moral issues • Considering questions of justice and social concern • Justifying one's own arguments • Reconsidering in the light of another's views	Is it ever all right to kill a living creature? If it is, under what circumstances? If not, why not? Is there a difference between killing an elephant and stepping on an ant? Is it ever right to use violence? Is there a moral difference between two men fighting in the street and two men fighting in a boxing ring? Should you give money to a beggar on the street? From a given list of rules to live your life by, which three are the most important? Do you treat some people differently to others? Why, and are you being fair?
Questions of faith (Theological Dialogue) • Reflecting on life's big questions • Expressing one's own convictions • Sharing and comparing different viewpoints	How did the world begin? How do you know? What do you think happens to people when they die? What do you think will happen to you? A good, hard-working boy has a terrible car accident that means he can't walk any more. Why has God let this happen? Do you believe in God? If so, what is God like? If not, why not? Do you believe in angels? If not, why not? If so, who are they and what do they do? What is the most precious gift that we, as human beings, have been given? How should we use it?

Dialogue skills

For some children, dialogue comes naturally. Faced with a computer screen and an e-mail from their partner, the ideas flow. Others need more help to keep the dialogue alive. This is where the teachers have an important enabling role to play. Pupils may need support at both ends of the dialogue exchange: initiating an exchange and formulating a response.

Initiating an exchange

We will look later at the role of classroom discussion in providing pupils with a bank of understandings and awareness of a range of views on which to draw when faced with the e-mailing task (page 30). As they proceed to write their e-mail, the teacher may wish to give them further prompts. The following is a checklist of key questions for pupils to ask themselves:

- Have I considered the needs of my partner?
- Have I offered my own views on the topics discussed?
- Have I given reasons to back up my views?
- Will my partner understand the words I am using?
- Have I given my partner a question or problem to think about?

Responding to an e-mail

Children are often so keen to put down their own ideas that they forget the importance of responding to the e-mail they have just received. As dialogue partners, they need to acknowledge the receipt of e-mails, comment on what has been written and answer questions that have been asked. Again prompts can be given for those who are finding the process difficult. Teachers may encourage pupils to organise their responses around the four dialogue skills of clarification, affirmation, disagreement and extension.

- Do you understand what your partner has written?
  If not, ask them to explain the difficult word or idea.
- Do you agree with anything your partner has written?
  If you do, let them know where your ideas are the same.
- Do you disagree with their ideas?
  If you do, explain why you think differently.
- Would you like to know more about their views on the subject?
  Give them a question that will make them think further.

Dialogue prompts

To support pupils in their e-mail dialogue, sentence starters such as the following can be given:

Clarification

When you said ... what did you mean?
I didn't understand what you meant by...
Can you tell me what ... is?
What do you mean by ... ?
Is ... the same as ... ?

Affirmation

I like your idea...
My ideas about ... are very similar to yours.
I agree with you when you say...
I think ... too.
We both think the same about...

Extension

What do you think about ... ?
If ... would you still think the same?
Does that mean you also think ... ?
What if ... ?
Do you think it would be the same if ... ?

Disagreement

I agree with you about ... but I don't think...
You said ... but I think...
I'm not sure about ... I think...
But if ... then ...
I can't agree with ... because...

Supporting quality e-mail dialogue

The teacher's role, therefore, is to ensure that the e-mail dialogue flows, that it is responsive and challenging. The following guidelines are designed to aid teachers in this task.

- **Response**: As they e-mail their partners, pupils should be encouraged to respond to the e-mails they have received. They may acknowledge the receipt of e-mails, comment on what has been written, answer some of the questions that have been asked.
- **Focus on topic**: Schools may have produced programmes of exchanges linking the e-mail activity to RE and Citizenship objectives. In order to fulfil these curriculum requirements it is important that e-mails focus on the topics being covered. Once the introductory e-mails have been sent, teachers may ask pupils to write about the topic focus first and end with more personal chat.
- **Exchange of information**: Exchanging information about each other's religious and cultural experiences and practices is one aim of the project. Pupils should be encouraged to be informative, to think of things they could tell their partner that they might not already know.
- **Comparison**: The exchanges are an opportunity for the children to explore the similarities and differences between their own and their partner's lives and viewpoints. They should be encouraged to compare their ideas and experiences.
- **Debate**: Another aim of the e-mail communication is the exchange and development of ideas. Pupils should be encouraged to express their personal opinions and beliefs about the questions of faith and ethics that they are discussing. They should try to back up their arguments with reasons. When reading the opinions expressed by their partners, they should consider whether or not they agree, and why.
- **Springboard**: Once they have responded to their e-mail, pupils should be encouraged to produce a springboard for further discussion, something for their partners to engage with. They could give them a key question, related to the topic, for them to consider. They might find that it is easier to discuss some broader issues by providing a brief case study from which general principles can be drawn.
- **Flow**: Over-concentration on spelling and punctuation can interrupt the flow of the e-mail dialogue. Unless errors make the writing incomprehensible or are just sloppy, teachers may decide to let them pass.
- **Avoid confidential information**: As they get to know their dialogue partner better, it is natural that children want more opportunities to converse with each other. However, pupils should be discouraged from exchanging confidential information such as detailed addresses, phone numbers or private e-mail addresses. This is an important teaching point for the children because of the dangers of such information being misused.

Examples of dialogue

We can gain a clearer idea of what constitutes quality dialogue by examining these examples of dialogical exchange between primary age children in Leicester, East Sussex and Birmingham schools.

An e-mail exchange between Year 5 pupils

To Anneka
I hope you are well. At school in RE we are thinking about god. What is the most precious gift that god has given me?
I think it is my family, relatives and my friend because if I didn't have them, I wouldn't have anybody to play and talk with.
I would like to know your ideas about this.
From Khadijah

Hello Khadijah
Thanks for your last e-mail. I think the most precious gift god has given me is his son Jesus who came down to earth and died on a cross for us so that we could be free of our sins.
In RE our topic is choices. What is the hardest choice that you have ever had to make?
On Monday we are going to have a class mass. We will have some bidding prayers, thank you prayers, a little bit of acting and we shall sing some hymns.
From Anneka

Dear Anneka
Thank you for your e-mail. We have got Jesus in our religion but he is not the son of god. We decrease our sins by praying five times a day. What does mass mean?
The hardest choice I have made in my life is whether I want to live in Preston or in Leicester. It is a hard choice for me because if I chose Leicester I would leave my friends behind, and if I chose Preston I wouldn't see my grandma very often or some of my cousins.
From Khadijah

These e-mails deal with two RE topics drawn from the schools' schemes of work: gifts and choices. They are to some extent responsive: questions are answered. Khadijah picks up a word she doesn't understand (mass) and asks for clarification. She also makes comparisons between her own and her partner's ideas about Jesus and about sins. Anneka does not comment, however, on Khadijah's choice of family and friends as her most precious gift.

Anneka does give an idea of some aspects of religious practice at a Catholic school. She needs to think more carefully about how easy it would be for a non-Christian to recognise some of the religious terminology she uses.

An e-mail exchange between Year 5 pupils

Dear Dan
Did you see the match last night with Man U? It was a really good goal but I don't think it was a penalty really what do you think? We've been doing about tigers in RE and this boy was killed by a tiger. We are asking the question is it ever all right to kill animals? I think it's all right to kill this tiger or he might kill someone else but I don't think you should kill animals, only if they hurt you. What do you think?
From Muhammad

Dear Muhammad
Thank you for your e-mail. I didn't see the match you wrote about so I don't know about the penalty. I agree with you that you shouldn't kill animals usually but I do eat meat so I suppose I can't say never kill animals. Do you eat meat? May be you could put the tiger in a cage so he won't hurt anyone.
From Dan

These e-mails follow the study in class of a report of an attack by a Bengal tiger on a young man in India. In the exchange the boys develop the argument, introducing questions that could form the basis of further class discussion. Muhammad raises the idea of self-defence as justification for taking animal life. Dan expresses some degree of agreement but takes the argument further by introducing the issue of vegetarianism. There is still some friend-to-friend sharing of personal interests but it doesn't get in the way of the main focus of the dialogue.

An e-mail exchange between Year 6 pupils

Dear friends
What do you think happens to us when we die? I think there is life after we die because ghosts are spirits and they come from us. I think life after death is OK because you can sit on clouds and float but you do miss home.
From Amy

Hello Amy
Thank you for your e-mail. We also think that there is life after death but we don't agree with you when you say ghosts are spirits and they come from us. We think their sort of demons and they come from fire. Also we think heaven is just so good that you can't miss home when you're there. Do you believe in hell? We believe good people go to heaven and bad people go to hell. They have to go across a bridge if it shakes you know you are going to hell and if it doesn't shake you know you will go to heaven. Do you believe there are stages in Heaven, if so what happens at the different stages?
From Aneesa and Humayra

These e-mails deal with the popular discussion point of life after death. Amy has very little religious background but it is still a topic about which she has ideas. She gives a reason for her belief in life after death based on the existence of ghosts. Her e-mail partners have read her comments carefully and respond directly to them. They both agree with her in part but also find areas of disagreement. Comparisons are made between their different views of life after death and the questions provide a springboard to further discussion.

An e-mail exchange between Year 3 pupils

Dear Bella
Are you celebrating Cristmas? We had an Eid party on Friday. We are having a party for Cristmas on Tjursday.
Love Amira

Dear Amira
Yes, we are celebrating Christmas.
I'm celebrating it with my family and my nan.
Are you celebrating Christmas with anyone?
Do you have any brothers and sisters?

I have a brother and a sister. My sister is 4 today. What is a Eid party.
From Bella

Dear Bella
Eid means that people share food and it's the end of Ramadan and fasting.
We are not celebrating Christmas because we are Tamil. I will be playing games with my brothers and sisters. I have one big sister called Fatima and a twin brother called Mohamed.
Love from Aysha.

These exchanges are at the sharing experiences and exchanging information stage of the e-mail programme. From a simple beginning the children have learned something about different festivals for different communities, about Christmas as a family occasion and Eid as the end of the fasting period of Ramadan. In her response to the last e-mail, Bella could ask for more information about the fasting season of Ramadan.

The exchanges are responsive, the children directly answering each other's questions.

Part of an e-mail exchange between Year 6 pupils

I think that when I die a new baby will be born and it will have my soul. What ideas do you have?
From James

That's a good idea James that would be nice if it did happen. Do you think your soul would remember who it was before.
Actually our ideas are different. We belive if people do bad things then they will go to hell, and if they do good things they will go to heaven. Heaven and hell are in the sky.
From Julehka and Shital

The girls' response to James' e-mail is a good example of how to value the views of others and yet disagree. They are encouraging him to extend his thinking further with the question about the soul's memory. It would be interesting to know whether James thought there was any difference in the fate of 'good' and 'bad' people after death.

In another e-mail James tells his partners that he is a Christian. Shital is a Hindu. Their thoughts about life after death illustrate the point that children don't necessarily share the conventional beliefs of the traditions with which they identify.

Setting up an e-mail link

Before the dialogue can begin, various organisational structures need to be in place. The co-ordinators of the project within the two schools need to be in regular contact as they organise the pairing of students and plan the programme of exchanges. Equally important to the success and continuation of the project is a solid base of support for each co-ordinator within their own school. This section offers step-by-step advice on the practicalities of setting up an e-mail link.

Step one: preparing the school for an e-mail link

Ethos: If the project is to gain the support of management and staff, the contribution it can make to the school in general, and to the children's learning in particular, needs to be recognised. In most schools the mission statement will back up arguments in favour of the project. E-mail dialogue fits in well with a school ethos committed to valuing diversity and promoting community links[1].

Management: The link will be given status if it is incorporated into the School Development Plan and the management of the school will be committed to providing the support (in terms of time, funding and training) to make sure it succeeds. It might be appropriate to appoint a link governor for the project who can take an active interest and make periodic reports to the full governing body.

Colleagues: All colleagues (teachers and teaching assistants) supporting children in the dialogue will need to be aware of the purposes of the exchanges. They may need training to support pupils in the development of e-mailing and dialogue skills. A project working party of colleagues can be set up to share the planning, monitoring and review.

Technology: Pupils will require regular access to e-mail facilities within school, whether in an ICT suite or in classrooms well supplied with computers. Support will be needed from the colleague in charge of ICT in the school (and from the school technician) in setting up the e-mail links and sorting out any technological difficulties that might occur.

Religious Education: The co-ordinator of Religious Education may well be the initiator of the project within the school. If this is not the case it is important that (s)he is involved in planning Religious Education objectives into the programme of exchanges and in monitoring the RE outcomes. Where there is a teacher responsible for citizenship it would be appropriate to ask for similar involvement.

Outside support: Promoting a project within one's own school community and rallying colleagues to the cause can be hard work. Outside support can give project co-ordinators that extra confidence, offering advice and keeping alive a broader picture of the project when it is in danger of getting lost in the details of internal school affairs. The school link may be part of a wider network of e-mail partnerships (such as the **building e-bridges** project). Local RE advisers and RE networks can also provide valuable support.

[1] As set out in 'The school curriculum and the National Curriculum: values, aims and purposes' by QCA in *The National Curriculum* (QCA, DfES, 1999)

Step two: choosing a partner school

Once they are assured of a firm base of support for their project within their own school, project co-ordinators and working parties can begin to consider their choice of partner school.

Difference: As a prime purpose of the e-mail link is encounter with difference, the teachers will want to find a partner school that contrasts sufficiently in location and demography with their own. Through careful pairing, a multi-cultural urban school can become the partner of a rural predominantly white school; children from a council estate (again largely white) can dialogue with Muslims from the inner city; Catholic children can share their views with Hindus and Sikhs.

Attitudes: An e-mail link may be a tool for combating pupil ignorance and prejudice towards a particular group. Teachers aware of pupils' negative attitudes towards Islam, for example, may seek out a partner school with a sizeable Muslim population; colleagues in some areas of the United Kingdom may wish to bridge a Catholic/Protestant divide; other prejudices might be dispelled by building friendships with students at a Special School.

Curriculum needs: Choices may also be influenced by curriculum needs. If a year group is making a detailed study of Christianity, contact with a church school may be welcome. A topic under the heading 'journeys' could be enhanced by sharing the hajj experience with children who have been on the pilgrimage themselves.

Location: Another consideration is the location of the partner school. Some schools look for local partners, from a contrasting area of the same city, for example. This has advantages in that teachers can get together easily to share planning or sort out any problems. Children, too, have the opportunity for joint trips and visits to each other's school. Others opt for partners in different regions of the country and so benefit from an added geographical dimension to the exchange, as they find out about another locality in the UK[2]. Joint residentials are an exciting possibility for face-to-face contact.

Service: Teachers might also like to consider what their school has to offer potential partners. A multi-cultural, multi-faith city school, for example, has a wealth of knowledge and experience to present as a resource to schools in small town or more rural locations. A school with a strong faith tradition or a vigorous RE department has valuable contributions to make to the religious learning of pupils in other establishments.

Contacts: Personal connections and friendships between teachers are often used to bring together different schools. Meetings between RE teachers at courses and conferences provide valuable opportunities for sounding out e-mail link possibilities. RE advisers can provide valuable assistance through their knowledge of schools, RE teachers and co-ordinators. They may be able to suggest valuable contacts for schools to follow up in their own or other authorities. Projects and networks of schools engaged in e-mail dialogue (such as **building e-bridges**) can help find partners for those interested in taking part.

[2] Geography programme of study, *The National Curriculum*

Step three: Sharing information about school and locality

Through e-mail dialogue, pupils are acquiring a contextualised understanding of religion; they are learning to relate people's viewpoints, beliefs and practices to their background, circumstances and experiences. Pupils can find out many of the contextual details through the question and answer of e-mail exchange, but it is useful at the outset to have some idea of the setting in which their partners are living and working. Teachers (particularly where time is short or the curriculum is loaded) might themselves collect materials and supply their link school with a variety of background information. Where possible the children should be involved in the collecting and processing of information themselves. In the process they will have the opportunity to develop several valuable learning skills:

- Reflecting on their community and their position within that community
- Selecting and creating resources to interest and inform their e-mail partners
- Formulating research questions as they seek information about their link school and its context
- Using a variety of sources (websites, maps, books, photographs, newspaper articles, tourist information)
- Classifying and sorting information from different sources to build up a picture of life in a particular locality
- Making decisions on how best to present that information

Information sharing could usefully form the focus of the first half term of the project before the dialogue begins.

Information sharing exercises

School prospectus: pupils design and create their own school prospectus in book or CD form

Photo gallery: digital cameras are used to build up a gallery of images of the school and locality

Hotspot map or plan: with ICT support, pupils incorporate these images into a map of the area, or a town or school plan, using hotspot links

Tourist brochure: pupils produce a tourist brochure of their own locality

Display: pupils combine what they have found out themselves and what their link school has sent to create a classroom or computer suite display as a visual backdrop to their e-mail activities

Step four: Pairing the pupils

The next stage in the setting up of the e-mail exchange is the pairing of individual pupils. The most fruitful dialogue partnerships are ones where there is both contrast and compatibility. There needs to be an element of difference and challenge, but at the same time enough common ground and shared understanding to make communication possible and friendship likely.

Faith background: Where partners have different faith backgrounds they will be able to learn about different practices and beliefs and engage with contrasting views. Dialogue will also reduce suspicion about those of other religious traditions. For many teachers this is the main purpose of the e-mail link.

Ethnic background: By providing opportunities for friendships to develop across racial and cultural difference, e-mail dialogue broadens pupils' experience and helps to break down prejudice.

Age: It is usually advisable for children of similar age to be e-mailing each other. The likelihood of shared educational experience and interest level is greater, thus making communication easier.

Ability: If there is a marked contrast of ability between e-mail partners, dialogue becomes difficult. Less able students may have problems reading and processing their partner's communication and the more able might get frustrated by the lack of challenge in their partner's contribution to the debate.

Interests: A shared interest or hobby, such as music or sport, might help children to relate to each other whatever their differences might be.

Numbers: It is unlikely that the two schools will have exactly the same numbers of children taking part in the e-mailing. Some of the children may need to work in twos e-mailing one child at the other school. Teachers may decide they would like their pupils to work in pairs anyway so that they can share ideas and discuss their e-mails together.

Gender: Schools will have to decide whether to have single or mixed gender partnerships. Many children prefer same gender friendships though an exact match is rarely possible as gender ratios vary from class to class. Teachers may wish to use the e-mailing experience as an opportunity for getting boys and girls to work with each other by deliberately organising mixed gender pairings. Another approach is to arrange the e-mailing so that a boy and girl pair at one school jointly e-mails a similar pair at the other.

'Turbulence': In some schools there is a high 'turbulence' factor with children leaving the school and arriving throughout the year. Others have a significant number of pupils on extended holidays with relatives abroad. Where this is an issue, a teacher might decide to have the children in her class working in twos (as above). If one of the pair should leave, their partner at the other school will not be left without an e-mail friend.

Language levels: If a child is a new arrival with limited English, they can work alongside another child who shares their language and work out their messages together.

In order to match the children with suitable partners, schools will need to share some of this basic information about their children. At the beginning of the project one of the schools will need to send an annotated class list (such as the one below) to its partner to be used in the pairing process.

Name	Gender	Year	Ability	Religious affiliation	Other relevant details
Jennifer	Female	5	Average to high	Christian (Methodist) Sunday School	African Caribbean/white; Skilled dancer
Abubaker	Male	6	High	Muslim – practising	Somali; spent most of life in Sweden; lives with aunt; parents in Somalia
Mark	Male	6	Average	None	Belongs to local football club
Krishna	Female	5	Low	Hindu	Gujarati; has learning support in class; big fan of pop group Blue
Ewa	Female	6	Average	Christian (Catholic)	Polish background; plays piano
Adrian	Male	5	High	Christian – doesn't attend church	Knows all there is to know about dinosaurs!

Step five: Setting up pupils' e-mail accounts

Another practicality of the project that needs sorting out as soon as possible is the assigning of e-mail addresses to the children. Various e-mail arrangements are used in schools. ICT co-ordinators and technicians will be able to advise colleagues on what is available in theirs. A class (or group of children within a class) may share an e-mail address. Child-to-child e-mail dialogue is still possible in these circumstances, though the names of the addressees need to be included very clearly in the title of each e-mail sent so that individual messages can be found easily in the general class inbox.

Other schools set up individual e-mail accounts for all pupils taking part. Each child will have a user name (it may be closely related to their own name and so easy to remember, or coded so it is harder for anyone other than the child and teacher to access) and a password which they keep secret from everyone except their teacher. This will prevent other children misusing their classmates' addresses to send inappropriate messages of their own which cannot be traced to the sender. It is a good idea for the teacher to keep a record of all user names and passwords in case the children forget them. Only the addresses need sending on to the partner school.

Name	User name	Password	E-mail address
Cole, Mark	MarkC	goal	MARKC@harnbury_jun.willingborough.sch.uk
Daud, Farah	FarahD	parrot	FARAHD@harnbury_jun.willingborough.sch.uk
Durgai, Krishna	KrishnaD	blue	KRISHNAD@harnbury_jun.willingborough.sch.uk
Hussain, Ahmed	AhmedH	eagle	AHMEDH@harnbury_jun.willingborough.sch.uk

It is useful for the teacher to be able to keep track of the exchanges, to check that all the e-mails have been sent, to know when e-mails from the other school arrive, and to evaluate the contents of the exchanges and progress of the dialogue. A separate project account can be set up for this purpose and the children taught to use the copy facility (Cc:) whenever they send their e-mails, as in this example.

To: MARKC@harnbury_jun.willingborough.sch.uk
Cc: REproject
Bcc:
Subject: All about me
Message:

Dear Mark

I am nine for three days. My birthday is on April 11th.

I live in Leicester which is a nice place to live because it has facilities for every religion, a good bus service and a good education.

I am a Muslim which means that I go to mosque every weekday from 5:00 to 7:30 and wear a scarf [head covering] whenever I go out [to cover my head] because of my religion.

I have one sister who is one and a half years older than me.

I was born in Nairobi, the capital city of Kenya, in South Africa. I migrated to England when I was two and a half years old.

I look forward to hearing from you.

From Ameera

Step six: Timetabling the programme of exchanges

The **building e-bridges** model of e-mail dialogue organises the exchanges into discrete units, between three and six periods of activity in a year. In this way the model encourages a more focused interchange, each unit having its own theme and purpose, and enables the teacher to incorporate the e-mail link into their Religious Education teaching programme. Classroom learning and discussion prepares the children for the e-mailing. Once the unit of e-mail exchange is complete, feedback of information and ideas generated by the dialogue can be used for follow-up work. If this interplay of classroom and e-mail work is to be effective, the programme needs to be carefully planned and adhered to as closely as possible. Another advantage of this model is that it keeps the children's interest in the e-mail link alive as they come fresh, after a break, to each new unit.

The needs of each school are different. Timetabling the exchanges might be influenced by a variety of factors such as residentials, school productions, exams. Early on in their joint planning of the project, project co-ordinators from the two schools will need to decide together how often and when the e-mailing is to take place.

Example 1

In this example, the schools take it in turn to initiate the exchange.
At the end of each unit, the children who began the exchange return to the suite to read the final message and share the outcomes of the dialogue in a class feedback session.

Unit 1

Week beginning	
3 November	School A
10 November	School B
17 November	School A
24 November	School B

Unit 2

12 January	School B
19 January	School A
26 January	School B
2 February	School A

Unit 3

1 March	School A
8 March	School B
15 March	School A
22 March	School B

Unit 4

7 June	School B
14 June	School A
21 June	School B
28 June	School A

Example 2

School C is working with two classroom computers and so needs more time to get through the e-mail exchanges. This timetable allows two weeks for each round of e-mails.

Unit 1

Week beginning	
3 & 10 Nov	School C
17 Nov	School D
24 Nov & 1 Dec	School C

Unit 2

12 Jan	School D
19 & 26 Jan	School C
2 Feb	School D

Unit 3

16 Feb & 1 Mar	School C
8 Mar	School D
15 & 22 Mar	School C

Unit 4

26 April	School D
3 & 10 May	School C
17 May	School D

Unit 5

7 & 14 June	School C
21 June	School D
28 Jun & 5 Jul	School C

Example 3 (Key Stage 3)

In this example, an RE class of Key Stage 3 pupils is studying Islam. The pupils themselves are mainly Christian or secular in their outlook. Their link school has a large number of Muslim students. Dialogue is set up between the two classes on key aspects of the faith, with opportunities for the pupils in the two schools to compare, contrast and comment. Between units there is a week timetabled in for organisation of thoughts on the particular topic.

Unit 1: God and Creation

Monday 12 January — School E
Wednesday 14 January — School F
Monday 19 January — School E
Wednesday 21 January — School F

Unit 2: The Prophet and his example

Monday 2 February — School E
Wednesday 4 February — School F
Monday 9 February — School E
Wednesday 11 February — School F

Unit 3: The Qur'an and revelation

Monday 1 March — School E
Wednesday 3 March — School F
Monday 8 March — School E
Wednesday 10 March — School F

Unit 4: Pilgrimage and the Five Pillars

Monday 22 March — School E
Wednesday 24 March — School F
Monday 29 March — School E
Wednesday 31 March — School F

Step seven: Planning for Religious Education outcomes

As schools make their initial contacts, one of the important items of information to share is the RE scheme of work for the year groups taking part. The teachers and RE co-ordinators then have the role of identifying valuable links between the programmes of work that the two sets of pupils will be following, in order to find themes for the e-mail dialogue exchanges. It may be that both schools are covering the same topic. If they are both studying Creation, for example, they can share and compare their views on the beginning of life and humankind's relationship to the rest of the created world. If Islam is the focus, non-Muslim children will be able to find out about particular beliefs and practices from the first-hand experiences of Muslim partners, and Muslim children will have to reflect on those beliefs and practices as they try to express and explain them to their friends. Even when the topics covered are not obviously the same, overlaps and links may be found.

Topic 1	Topic 2	Possible links
Sikhism	Christianity	Leaders and discipleship, what makes a good leader, whom we follow, why and how we show our loyalty; sacred texts, books special to us
Hinduism	Journeys	Stages on life's journey, the duties at each stage; where have we come from and where are we going? (link with rebirth); pilgrimage to special places (Varanasi)
Signs and symbols	Creation	Finding symbols from the natural world, for example power, fear, loyalty, perseverance, beauty, infinity; looking for signs of God in the natural world – are they convincing?
Pentecost	Islam	Messages, being a witness; what message would we like to share with the world?; would the world listen? Establishing a community – what keeps it together?
Worship	Buddhism	Prayer and meditation – is there a difference? What happens when people pray or meditate? Aids for meditation or prayer – what would you find helpful?
Justice	Death	Does the way we have lived our life make a difference to us when we die? God's justice, punishment and reward – is there a conflict between forgiveness and justice? (Do bad people automatically get punished?) Is there any reason for being good if you don't believe in Hell ?

Dialogue grid

A clear plan of the dialogue programme makes life easier for teachers as they work through it and also serves as evidence of the objectives being covered.

In this example of a planning format, the exchanges are organised into the different stages of dialogue, RE and Citizenship objectives are clearly set out, and some idea is given of the kinds of questions the pupils could be expected to ask. The contents of such a grid need to be negotiated between project co-ordinators (or working groups) of the two schools. It may be that they share out responsibility for the different units.

Date	**November**	**January**	**March**	**June**
RE topics	Introduction	Christianity – baptism Life's journey – birth	Christianity – Easter Life's journey – death	Relationships Leaders – Gandhi and Martin Luther King
Stage of dialogue	**Introduction**	**Sharing Experience**	**Questions of Faith**	**Ethical Debate**
Questions	What are your favourite subjects at school? What are you good at? What do you like doing in your spare time? Do you like living where you do? – pros and cons Have you always lived there?	Do you have a baby in your family? What preparations do families make for a new baby? How is the name chosen? How is the baby welcomed into the family or faith community? Why is it important to welcome the baby in this way?	What do you believe happens when people die? Does it make any difference if they've been good or bad in their life? Do you think dying is the worst thing that can happen to anyone? Can people come back after they've died?	Use case studies including examples from lives of Gandhi and MLK. Is it ever justifiable to use violence against another person? In what circumstances? If someone is hurting you should you fight back? What if they were hurting someone else? Is war always wrong?
RE expectations	To compare their own and other people's lives. To recognise what is important to other people.	To respond to others' experiences. To compare experiences. To make links between beliefs and ceremonies.	To reflect on life's 'big questions'. To recognise different responses to those questions. To express their own convictions.	To think and respond to another's opinions. To back up own opinions with reasons. To make links between principles and actions. To make links between religious beliefs and principles that guide actions.
Citizenship or PSHE expectations	To recognise their worth as individuals identifying positive achievements 1b[3] To think about the lives of other people 4b To develop relationships 5f	To think about people with different values and customs 4b To be aware of different types of family relationships 4c To recognise cultural and religious differences and similarities between people 4f	To reflect on spiritual and moral issues 2e To be sensitive to feelings and other points of view 4a	To explain their views on issues that affect themselves and society 1a To debate topical issues 2a To consider moral and social dilemmas 5g To realise the consequences of aggressive behaviour 4d

[3] The numbers given refer to Citizenship guidelines for Key Stage 2, *The National Curriculum 1999*

Timetable for setting up the e-mail dialogue link

This suggested timetable shows how preparation for the e-mail dialogue might be spread across the summer and first half of the autumn terms. It can serve as a checklist that everything is in place.

Summer term

- Idea of project approved by ICT and RE Co-ordinators and school management ____________
- Project incorporated into school (or departmental) Improvement Plan ____________
- Project group of interested colleagues set up ____________
- Partner school identified and approached ____________
- Lines of communication set up between schools (for example, exchange of co-ordinators' e-mail addresses) ____________
- Project link governor appointed ____________

Autumn term

Before half-term

- Pupils paired off with e-mail partners in the link school ____________
- Pupils given e-mail accounts ____________
- Project e-mail account set up ____________
- Timetable of exchanges agreed between schools ____________
- Schemes of work shared and common themes found ____________
- Dialogue planning grid completed ____________
- Information about the schools and their localities collected, researched and shared ____________

E-mailing begins after half-term

Running the e-mail link

Organising the class

There are a number of different models of classroom organisation and staff deployment to suit the circumstances of the individual school. Whatever model the teachers choose for their pupils, there needs to be a combination of flexibility and support, so children can express and develop their own views, and teachers supply suggestions and prompts should they be finding the process difficult. Below are some possible models which illustrate the variety of models used in various school partnerships.

Model A: Whole class e-mailing together

The school has an ICT suite with fifteen computers. The pupils each have their own e-mail partner but sit in pairs.

The teacher begins the lesson with a reminder of the theme that they have been covering in class and a warm-up discussion session. The pupils open up their e-mails one after the other, then discuss the contents and possible responses together before the child to whom the e-mail is addressed types in her reply. At the end of the lesson the children feed back to the whole class and compare some of the ideas they have developed during the session.

With this model the whole class works together and the children are able to get through the e-mail exchange within a fairly limited period.

Model B: Children working a few at a time

E-mail sessions are timetabled for an afternoon when there is an extra member of staff to work with the pupils. An independent activity is set up for the class supervised by one teacher (or teaching assistant). The other teacher takes a group of children into the ICT suite to work on their e-mails and gives them individual support. As they finish, the children return to class and other classmates take their place.

Using this model, children can work at their own pace. The teacher is able to decide what number he can work with most productively. Whole class input and discussion on the themes of the exchange takes place in the classroom beforehand and there is a rounding-up session back in class at the end of the afternoon.

Model C: E-mail dialogue run as a lunchtime club

This model is used in a school where there are timetabling difficulties with the ICT suite. In the e-mailing week the pupils have access to the suite at lunchtime and staff share responsibility for supporting the dialogue and checking the e-mails as they are sent. The children respond well to the extra independence they are given as they organise their lunch hours to accommodate the e-mailing. The discussion around the themes of the exchange takes place within the RE class beforehand. The teachers can decide whether to have a whole year group involved in the exchange or just a committed group who will feed back what they have learned to the rest of their classmates.

Model D: Using a limited number of computers within the classroom

The RE lesson takes place at the beginning of the week. The children brainstorm the topic they are studying, decide what they would like to find out, consider possible debating points, think of questions they could ask. They make notes which they can use when it is their turn to e-mail. During the afternoon sessions over a couple of weeks, the children take it in turns to use the two computers in the classroom, referring to their notes to help them. The teacher and teaching assistant make sure to check the e-mails before they are sent. This model is not ideal as there is a long time lag between the initial discussion and the final e-mail but it does enable a school with more limited ICT facilities to participate.

Model E: For classes with limited project time and limited ICT facilities

The following model is designed for an eight-week project where input from students at a partner school will be used to support class work. It is suitable for a Key Stage 3 class. Pupils use lunch hour time to send initial e-mails which introduce themselves and give some idea of their faith position. They are then divided into four groups, each with a particular aspect of the topic to focus on. In the first two weeks the first group sends and receives two e-mails and contributes their findings to the work the rest of the class is doing. The next group then takes over the e-mailing around their focus, and so on until the project is complete.

Organising the learning

The most valuable e-mailing experiences are those where the dialogue is tied in closely with classroom learning. Ideally the exchanges should both feed on and feed back into the curriculum. If children have been given some stimulus for dialogue before the exchanges begin, thoughts will flow more easily. Pupils should also be given an opportunity to process what their partners have sent, to organise, analyse and reflect on those contributions so that their own understanding is enhanced.

To maintain a close relationship between lesson delivery and e-mail content, the dialogue can be included as an important component in medium- and short-term Religious Education planning, as in these examples:

Short-term planning example

Context: A school with a mix of religions (including Hindu, Sikh, Muslim, Christian, secular) e-mailing a predominantly white school where most identify as Christian but few have church involvement.
This is the plan for a follow-up lesson after an e-mail exchange on life after death.

Year Group: 4 **Topic**: Death **Focus**: Life after death

Lesson objectives: to understand that people have different ideas about the big question 'What happens to us when we die?'
To make comparisons between own and other people's points of view.

Resources: Copies of e-mail replies from partners to questions about what happens when we die.
Cards, pens, paper, whiteboards and so on.

Introduction: Revision of earlier work.
Working in pairs, think up one of life's 'big questions'; write on whiteboard.
Display questions to rest of class. From the 'big questions' draw out theme of life after death.

Activity: Working in groups, share copies of e-mail replies.
Use a highlighter to mark the section of the e-mail that relates directly to the question.
Write these answers onto the cards.
With your partner, sort the cards into statements you don't agree with and statements that you do, and discuss why.
Class feedback.
Write on a piece of paper: What happens when we die? My Ideas

Plenary: Divide board into different sections with large headings, for example: Death is the end; Going to another place; Being born again. Children stick their pieces of paper in the appropriate sections.
View board and consider majority views overall and majority views in the class.
Share some of the children's writing.

Evaluation: Based on feedback to class following discussion.
Children's writing.

Medium-term planning example

Context: A school with no Muslim pupils linked to a school with many Muslims.
This plan shows how the e-mailing becomes an integral part of the children's learning.

Year Group: 5 **Term:** Spring **Topic**: Islam (part 1)

Focus: What is a Muslim?

RE skills	**Responding**: expressing opinions and ideas (lesson 1) **Investigating**: asking appropriate questions and seeking evidence (lessons 2, 4) **Evaluating**: using evidence, reaching conclusions (lesson 5) **Synthesising**: linking ideas from a variety of sources, making connections (lesson 5) **Analysing**: identifying distinctive features of the religion (lessons 1, 5) **Empathising**: relating to experiences, thoughts, beliefs of others (lessons 3, 5)
Cross-curricular skills	**Communication and information technology**: e-mail dialogue **Working with others**: class and group discussion, e-mail partners **Enquiry skills**: asking relevant questions **Information-processing skills**: collecting relevant information, sorting, comparing, contrasting, analysing part/whole relationships

Lesson One (1 hour)

In groups: brainstorm the word ***Muslim***.
Feed back and look for common choices.
Individually represent in picture form what the word 'Muslim' means to you (avoid pictures of humans).
Plenary: share some of the pictures. Evaluate.
Discuss 'Where have we heard the word Muslim used?' 'How is it used?' 'Positively?' 'What would be the best way of finding out more about what it means to be a Muslim?'

Lesson Two – ICT (1 hour)
E-mailing

Respond to last e-mail.
Share news of Christmas break.
Ask e-mail partners for their answers to 'What is a Muslim?'

Lesson Three (1 hour)

Read the story of the life of the Prophet.
In pairs, produce a timeline of the Prophet's life.
Use the timeline to create a Fortune Line showing ups and downs of the Prophet's life in graph form (see *Thinking Through Religious Education* by Vivienne Baumfield).
Plenary: discuss, 'What is it about the Prophet's life that makes him so important to Muslims today?'

Lesson Four – ICT (1 hour)
E-mailing

Consider responses to the question, 'What is a Muslim?' Print them.
Compare what is written with own belief, experience and practice.
Ask questions for clarification or extension.

Lesson Five (1 hour)

In groups, share cards showing a variety of partners' e-mail responses to the question about being a Muslim.
Distinguish between practice and belief – sort cards into these categories.
Sort the cards into two piles: a) Muslims only (for example, 'follow the Prophet Muhammad (pbuh)', 'pray the Qur'an'); b) Muslims and others (for example, 'pray to God', 'are thoughtful and caring').
Discuss similarities and differences between being a Muslim and being a practitioner of another faith (or none).
Individually, represent in picture form what the word 'Muslim' means in the light of the e-mail responses.
Plenary: Compare the pictures with those of Lesson One. Any changes?
From the responses, pick out a few key areas for more detailed research and study on Islam.

Other examples of integrating classroom and e-mail dialogue

Classroom preparation for, and follow up to, the e-mail exchanges could include:

- **Brainstorming** words or topics to create a bank of ideas and meanings from which children can draw when e-mailing (for example a group of children brainstorm the word 'angel' before discussing beliefs about these beings with their partners).
- **Formulating searching questions** that will encourage partners to supply interesting information, explain practice, reflect carefully on the issues being discussed (for example 'What difference does praying make to your life?').
- **Creating lists** for partners to choose from or put in order of importance (for example 'Choose the three most important from a list of ten rules for community living and explain your choice').
- **Sharing a case study** for partners to consider and discuss (see below).
- **Sharing a story or a film** for pupils at both schools to discuss and make comments on. There are plenty of thought-provoking stories to share in this way and the study of films agreed and viewed by both classes can add a new dimension.
- **Using a comparison chart** to organise information or ideas received by e-mail under headings such as 'my experience', 'my partner's experience', 'shared experience', or 'my views on X', 'my partner's views on X', 'where we agree about X'.
- **Ordering, sorting, classifying** exercises with cards on which key statements and ideas from e-mails have been written (see planning examples above).
- **Writing a biographical sketch** of your e-mail partner.
- **Building up a class display** on the RE theme being studied and adding new reflections or information to the display as they arrive from e-mail partners.

Case study for ethical debate

Mrs Suleman has been left a lot of money, enough to pay for one of the following:

- an operation to make her daughter walk again;
- a beautiful holiday home on a Caribbean island;
- a new mosque in her community;
- a wood which developers want to cut down, destroying many trees, rare flowers and the habitat of thousands of creatures;
- enough medicine to cure ten people in an African country from an illness which could kill them;
- the rebuilding of a school for 200 pupils after it was destroyed in an earthquake.

How do you think she should spend her money, and why?

RE dialogue from film

Agnieszka Holland's *The Secret Garden* (Key Stage 2)

- How do the characters change during the film and why?
- Why is this an especially good film to share at Easter time?
- What does Mary mean when she says at the end of the film, 'If you look the right way, you can see that the whole world is a garden'? What is the right way?

Tim Burton's *Edward Scissorhands* (Key Stage 4)

- Was Edward a robot or a human, and what's the difference?
- Is the film a fairy story or a parable? Explain.

Maintaining the link

In order to ensure the continuity of the project, there needs to be commitment in both schools. The teachers involved will have so many demands on their time that it is easy for initial enthusiasm to wane. Through regular communication, colleagues can encourage each other and maintain interest in the project, thereby ensuring its success. At the same time children should be taught the importance of working at a friendship to keep it going. Here are a few hints for keeping the dialogue on course.

- From the outset of the project, establish lines of regular communication between the project co-ordinators at both schools. E-mail communication is clearly the most appropriate and the most straightforward but it is no use unless the co-ordinators view and respond to their e-mails regularly and often (that is, at least twice a week).
- Use these lines of communication to let the other school know when your pupils have sent a batch of e-mails through. This will serve as a prompt for the other school to get started with the replies.
- In between e-mailing sessions it helps to keep the relationship alive if you occasionally share some other activity the children have been involved in. E-mail photographs of school productions or outings, for example, or the occasional piece of work by the children in your class (for example a poem, a story, a piece of artwork).
- Send minutes of any project group meetings to the partner school so that colleagues have an overview of the project's progress on both sides of the link.
- Use a project group within your own school to make sure that the dialogue continues even if the teacher usually responsible for overseeing the e-mailing is away.
- If the computers are temporarily out of action, carry on the dialogue by other means (fax or ordinary mail) until they are back on line. The ICT is being used to facilitate dialogue; it should not be allowed to obstruct it if it goes wrong.
- If a child is away and misses an e-mail session, make sure the partner at the other end receives a message of some kind when they open their e-mail. It could be a note from the teacher informing him that his partner is away, or another member of the class could step in as a substitute and e-mail this child as well as their own partner.
- Impress on the children the importance of getting their e-mails finished on time and sent through to their partners, even if they write only a couple of lines. They should be able to empathise with the disappointment their partner would feel if they opened their e-mail account and found no message waiting for them.

Supervising the e-mails

An aim of this form of dialogue is to encourage a positive attitude to people of different backgrounds and traditions, and to build up cross-cultural, cross-faith friendships. The whole project would be undermined if unkind or insensitive messages got through. We are also well aware of the possibilities of abuse of electronic communication by unscrupulous adults. For this reason e-mail security is a pressing issue.

Acceptable use policy

Some schools have an 'acceptable use' policy for e-mail and the Internet which is shared and signed by teachers, parents and pupils. If you do not have one already in your school, you may consider adopting one. Advice on these AUPs can be found at www.ictadvice.org.uk.[1]

Filtering e-mail

Another security measure adopted by some schools and LEAs is a filtering system such as Symantec's *Mail-Gear* management application (www.symantec.com), to filter incoming and outgoing messages and attachments for inappropriate material. The text is checked against the authority's own dictionary of unsuitable words, and messages which contain them are diverted to the network administrator. Though this may add to the security of the e-mailing, it will not filter out all the possible areas of sensitivity and misunderstanding that can arise from discussions of religious belief and practice.

Supervised e-mailing

The LEA in which you work may have its own policy for e-mail security which affects the practice in your school. Nevertheless, whatever security systems you have in place, the only fail-proof safeguard against inappropriate communication is supervised e-mailing. All the e-mails need checking by a responsible adult before they are sent.

E-mail security guidelines

These guidelines may be helpful for those supervising e-mail dialogue:

- All e-mails sent between pupils need to be checked to make sure there is nothing there that might be offensive or hurtful to the e-mail partner.
- Though they may disagree with others' beliefs and views, pupils must not make comments that denigrate any group of people (religious, ethnic, cultural, and so on).
- Pupils must not make negative comments about people or things that are of great importance to their partner (family members; gods, prophets and religious leaders; holy scriptures; religious symbols and objects, and so on).
- All the children's e-mailing should take place within a properly safeguarded school system that outsiders cannot access.
- Parents' permission should be sought before close-up photographs of their children are sent to partner schools.
- Children must not share their home addresses, e-mail addresses or telephone numbers with their partners in case these get into the wrong hands.

[1] If you wish to view examples used by other schools, you can visit the following websites:
Ambleside C E Primary School (www.ambleside.schoolzone.co.uk/ambleweb/ourrules.htm);
Highcliffe Primary School (www.highcliffe.leics.sch.uk/information/internet.htm);
North Chadderton Secondary School (www.webschool.org.uk/aup.htm)

Evaluating the e-mail project

At the end of the project, teachers will want to evaluate its success. The main criterion for success is the contribution the project has made to the children's understanding and learning. What is needed is an assessment of the way the experience of the project has affected their thinking and attitude, increased their knowledge about other places, communities and traditions, and helped develop the skills of e-mailing and of dialogue. This grid suggests four focuses for evaluation and some possible assessment activities that the children could take part in. Project Co-ordinators are advised to keep samples of e-mails and work as evidence of the learning that has taken place.

Where there is a project link governor it would be appropriate for that governor to view the material being collected as a record of the learning taking place. The governor might also come into school during an e-mail session to view the children at work or to discuss the project with a group of them.

Project evaluation	Children's learning
Focus	*Method*
What are the children's thoughts about the project and what do they think they have learned?	Class discussion, group discussion or individual questionnaire for the children to complete: • What have they learned from the project? • Have they changed their ideas as a result of the project? • Would they recommend the project to others? If so, on what grounds? If not, why not? • How could the project be improved?
Has the project contributed to the children's learning in a particular aspect(s) of RE or Citizenship?	Teachers or project groups do an analysis of some of the exchanges to examine: • the clarity of the pupils' expression of their own ideas and the quality of the questions asked; • how far they have moved children's thinking forward in ethical debate, questions of faith and so on. Teachers look at examples of follow-up classwork to determine the contribution to learning made by e-mail exchange. Pupils write a biographical sketch of their e-mail partner – family, hobbies, beliefs, opinions, and so on. In the sketch they make comparisons with their own position.
Have the children been able to learn about another city or locality in the UK?	A sample of e-mails received by all the children is put together as a picture of the partner school's locality. This may be in a booklet, a display or a CD. Pupils produce a 'Same' and 'Different' chart to compare the localities. Pupils design a tourism poster of the locality, distilling some of the information they have collected over the year.
Have the children's ICT skills improved during the project?	Pupils have a list of the different ICT skills they will be using during the project and tick them off when they have been achieved. These might include: Opening, replying to, sending an e-mail; sending attachments; taking and sending digital photos, using a webcam

Once the evidence has been collected, the project group and project governor can have an end of year review meeting in which they examine the evidence and ask themselves:

- How has the project benefited the children?
- How has the project benefited the wider school?
- What problems has the project encountered over the last year?
- How can the project be improved or developed over the next year?

A project report around these questions can then be fed to the partner school, to other colleagues and to governors so that all are well informed.

Two models of biographical sketches for evaluation of learning

My e-mail friend

Jennifer is my e-mail friend. She is the same age as me but she was born in April and I was on June 10th. She lives with her mother and with her baby brother in a small village by the sea called X in the south by the sea. I have a little brother too. Jennifer likes reading and she has read the Harry Potter books like me. Her other hobby is swimming. She has got some swimming awards at the swimming bath but she also swims in the sea when it is warm.

I go swimming with school but I am not nearly as good as Jennifer is. She wears jeans and skirts. I sometimes wear jeans but I always have to wear clothes on my legs. I wear a headscarf but she doesn't.

Jennifer is a Christian and I am a Muslim. She hardly goes to church though but she went for her brother's christening and for the school's Christmas play. The church she goes to is old and has stained glass windows. I go to mosque school every day so that is different from Jennifer too. We don't have plays and we don't have christenings because I am Muslim.

Christening is when someone (a baby) is made a Christian and has a name. They have water put on them and they get a candle to show they have to shine like a light. I wasn't made a Muslim I just was born a Muslim. My granddad whispered Allah's name in my ear.

Jennifer thinks the greatest gift she has been given is the sun because if you didn't have the sun you wouldn't have light and heat and there would be no life so if there was no sun you wouldn't be alive to get gifts anyway. I agree that the sun is important but for me the Qur'an is the most important.

Ripesh	How we are the same	Me
He lives in Leicester, a busy city. He can speak Gujarati. His Mum was born in Kenya. He likes to play as a striker. He can play tabla drums.	Year 5, 10 years old. Both have a sister. Both like Science in school. Both like football.	I have a brother. My Mum was born in Ireland. I am goalie in the school team. I'm learning to play the guitar.
He celebrates Diwali and he has fireworks at night and Indian food. His family visits the temple and his Dad writes in an account book to get good luck for his business. He has lots of gods.	We celebrate festivals. Both celebrate Christmas and have presents and a tree at home.	I go to church at Christmas at midnight. Lots of candles and little statues of the Christmas story about Jesus. Jesus is our God.
His mum says when people die they come back and are born again in another body. He thinks his mum might be right.	We both think there's probably a heaven people go to when they die. Heaven is a place where everyone is happy and there's no bad, no war.	I believe in heaven for good people and even for bad because God will forgive if they say sorry. I believe my gran is in heaven but sometimes she comes back in dreams.
He thinks you shouldn't kill animals even for eating.	We both think you should be kind to animals because we are animals too. We both think it's alright to kill mosquitoes and headlice and small things that hurt us.	I think you can kill animals for eating because it's natural and animals kill other animals. But you shouldn't kill them in a cruel way.

Frequently asked questions

Will the e-mail link take up too much of my teaching time?

Once the project has been set up it will not take a great deal of teaching time. Arranged in discrete units with breaks in between, the exchanges themselves need take up only eight ICT sessions during the year. The outcomes of these exchanges can then be used to support, rather than detract from, class work.

The pupils at my school are really prejudiced in their views about people of other races and religions. Wouldn't they have the wrong attitude for inter-faith dialogue?

Yours is exactly the kind of school where such an e-mail project is needed. The careful supervision of the e-mailing situation provides a controlled environment in which your pupils can learn to relate positively to those of other cultures.

Most of my pupils have no background in religion. Will they be able to join in an inter-faith dialogue?

Whatever their religious background, whether or not they identify with any faith tradition, children can take part in Religious Education on an equal footing; issues of morality, 'big questions' such as how our world began and what happens when we die, are of equal interest to those who have and those who don't have a faith. Just as dialogue between different faith traditions helps to break down barriers, so does dialogue between religious and secular perspectives.

I'm not very confident with ICT. Will I be able to cope?

Any teacher taking part in an e-mail project is urged to make sure of the support of their ICT colleagues. However, basic e-mailing is not a very difficult skill to acquire. More ICT components can be fed into the project as and when the teacher feels confident with the e-mailing facility.

I've done e-mailing to another school with my class before but it was hard to keep up the initial momentum, e-mails became sporadic and everyone lost interest. What's to stop this happening again?

The e-mail model set out in this book is designed to keep up the momentum. It is designed to take place in short bursts with breaks in between. This should keep the freshness of the project. The programme of exchanges is also fed in to RE/Citizenship objectives and so has a definite purpose.

I would really like to take part in an e-mail dialogue but I teach in Key Stage 1. Are my pupils too young for the project?

The pupil-to-pupil model of dialogue is probably too demanding for Key Stage 1 pupils but you might like to consider setting up a class-to-class e-mail link instead, whereby the e-mail message is constructed as a whole class activity and sent to another class in a partner school. For the children this would be good preparation for a fuller involvement in Key Stage 2.

Notes